Theme Skills Tests
Table of Contents

Tests begin at Theme 2 for this level.

Colors All Around

Level K, Theme 2
Theme Skills Test Record

Student ______________________________ Date ________________

Test Record Form

PART	SCORE	LEVEL OF RESPONSE	RESULT S, D, E, or NE	COMMENTS
A Beginning Sounds (Maximum Score = 5)		4–5 = Strong 2–3 = Developing 1 = Emerging 0 = Not Evident		
B Sequence of Events (Maximum Score = 3)		3 = Strong 2 = Developing 1 = Emerging 0 = Not Evident		
C Making Predictions (Maximum Score = 3)		3 = Strong 2 = Developing 1 = Emerging 0 = Not Evident		
D Initial Consonants: *s, m, r* (Maximum Score = 5)		4–5 = Strong 2–3 = Developing 1 = Emerging 0 = Not Evident		
E High-Frequency Words: *I, see* (Maximum Score = 3)		3 = Strong 2 = Developing 1 = Emerging 0 = Not Evident		

Name

Beginning Sounds

Practice

1.

2.

3.

Go on

4.

5.

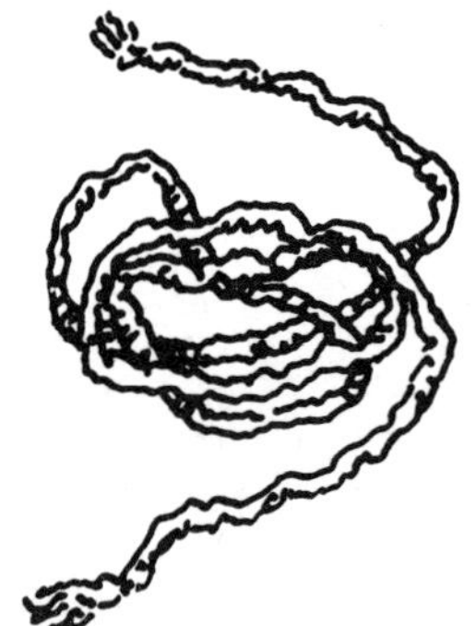

Part A Beginning Sounds ________

Name ______________________________

Sequence of Events

Practice

1.

2.

3.

Part B Sequence of Events ________

C Name ____________________

Making Predictions

1.

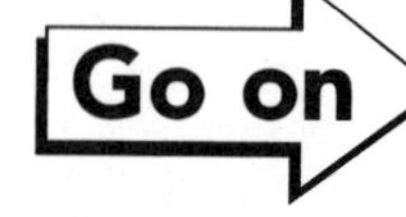

2.

3.

Part C Making Predictions ________

Name ____________________

Initial Consonants: *s, m, r*

Practice

1.

s

2.

r

2

3.

m

Go on

4.

r

5.

s

STOP

Part D Initial Consonants: *s*, *m*, *r* ________

Name ____________________

High-Frequency Words

Practice

I

see

1.

see

I

2.

I

see

3.

see

I

Part E High-Frequency Words: *I*, *see* ________

We're a Family

Level K, Theme 3

Theme Skills Test Record

Student ______________________________ Date ____________________

Test Record Form

PART	SCORE	LEVEL OF RESPONSE	RESULT S, D, E, or NE	COMMENTS
A Blending Onset and Rime Segmenting Onset and Rime (Maximum Score = 4)		4 = Strong 2–3 = Developing 1 = Emerging 0 = Not Evident		
B Story Structure: Characters/Setting (Maximum Score = 3)		3 = Strong 2 = Developing 1 = Emerging 0 = Not Evident		
C Drawing Conclusions (Maximum Score = 3)		3 = Strong 2 = Developing 1 = Emerging 0 = Not Evident		
D Initial Consonants: *t, b, n* (Maximum Score = 5)		4–5 = Strong 2–3 = Developing 1 = Emerging 0 = Not Evident		
E High-Frequency Words: *my, like* (Maximum Score = 3)		3 = Strong 2 = Developing 1 = Emerging 0 = Not Evident		

Name ______________________________

Blending Onset and Rime

Practice

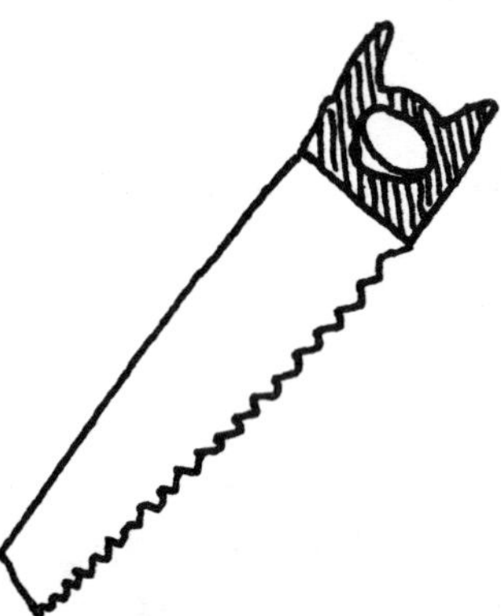

1.

2.

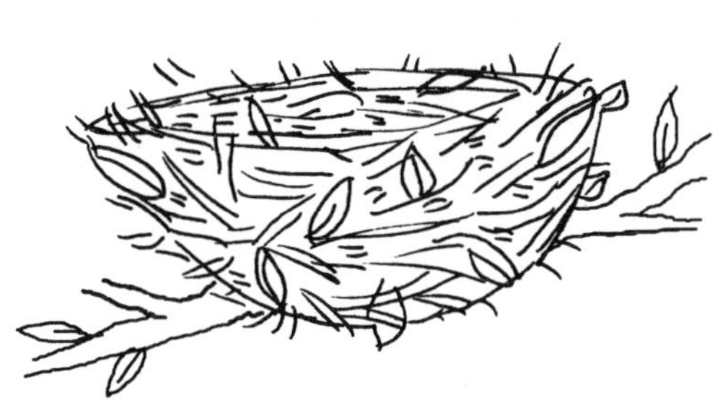

Part A Blending Onset and Rime ________

Segmenting Onset and Rime

Practice

Go on

3.

4.

Part A Segmenting Onset and Rime ________

B

Name ________________________________

Story Structure: Characters/Setting

1.

2.

3.

STOP

Part B Story Structure: Characters/Setting ________

C

Name____

Drawing Conclusions

1.

2.

3.

STOP

Part C Drawing Conclusions ________

Name ______________________________

Initial Consonants: *t*, *b*, *n*

1.

2.

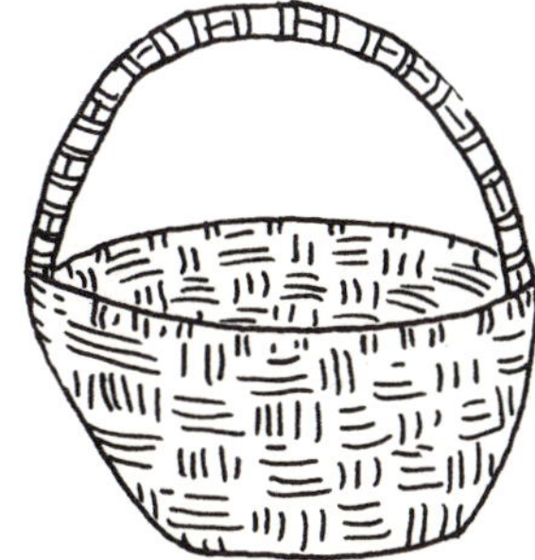

3.

n

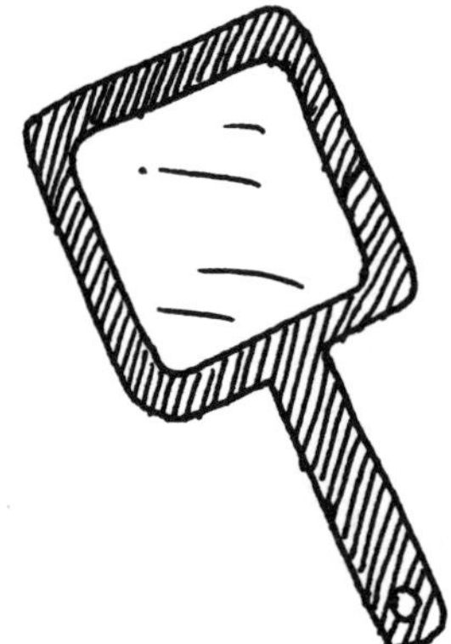

4.

b

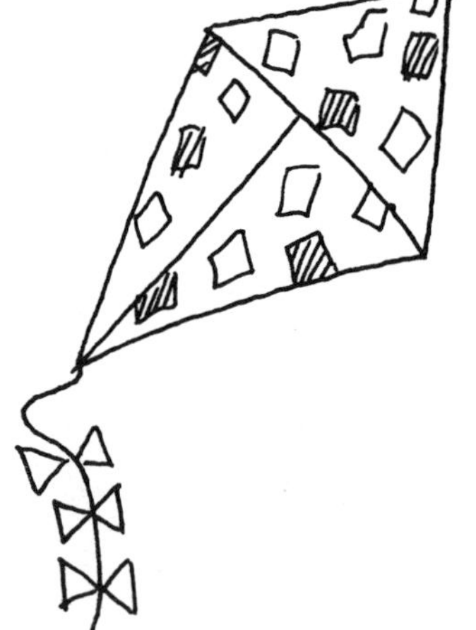

Go on

5.

n

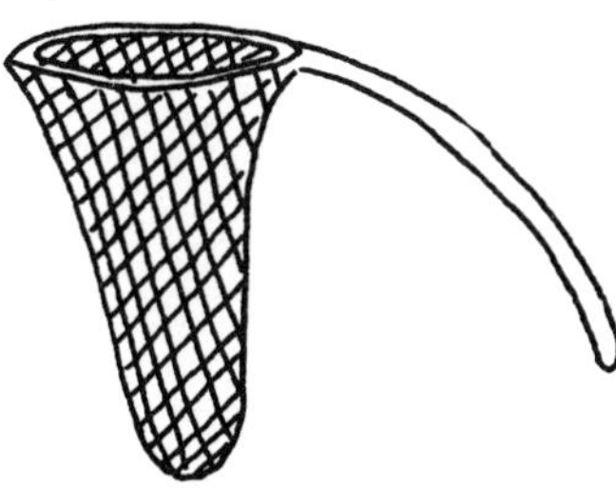

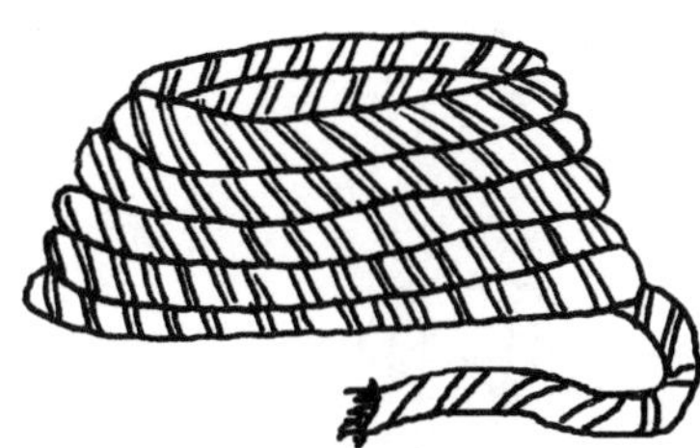

Part D Initial Consonants: *t*, *b*, *n* ________

Name____

High-Frequency Words

1\.

my

like

2\.

like

my

3.

my

like

Part E High-Frequency Words: *my, like* ________

Friends Together
Level K, Theme 4
Theme Skills Test Record

Student ______________________________ Date ________________

Test Record Form

PART	SCORE	LEVEL OF RESPONSE	RESULT S, D, E, or NE	COMMENTS
A Blending and Segmenting Onset and Rime Blending Phonemes (Maximum Score = 5)		4–5 = Strong 2–3 = Developing 1 = Emerging 0 = Not Evident		
B Text Organization and Summarizing (Maximum Score = 3)		3 = Strong 2 = Developing 1 = Emerging 0 = Not Evident		
C Cause and Effect (Maximum Score = 3)		3 = Strong 2 = Developing 1 = Emerging 0 = Not Evident		
D Initial Consonants: *h, v, c;* Blending Short *a* words (Maximum Score = 5)		4–5 = Strong 2–3 = Developing 1 = Emerging 0 = Not Evident		
E High-Frequency Words: *a, to* (Maximum Score = 3)		3 = Strong 2 = Developing 1 = Emerging 0 = Not Evident		

Name ____________________

Blending and Segmenting Onset and Rime

1.

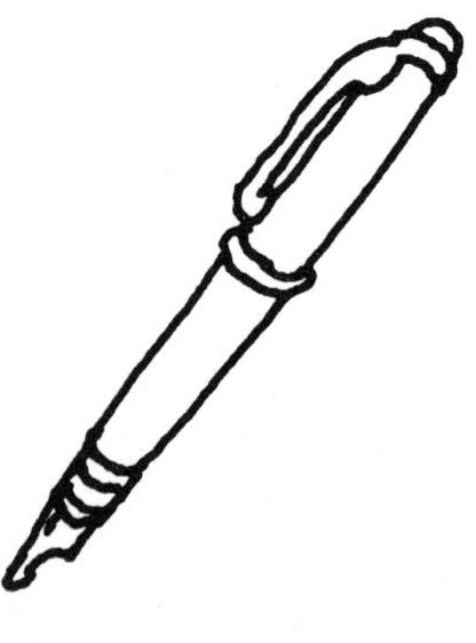

2.

3.

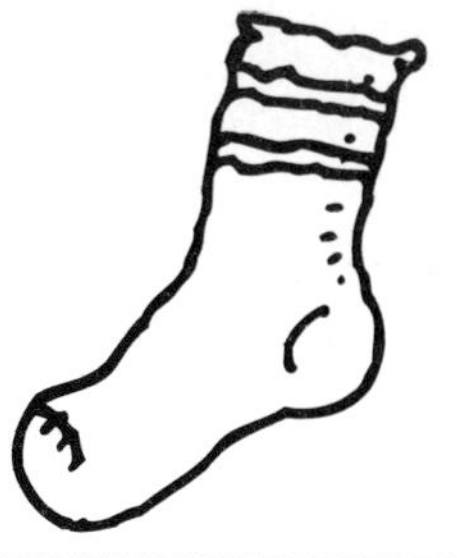

Part A Blending and Segmenting Onset and Rime ________

Blending Phonemes

Practice

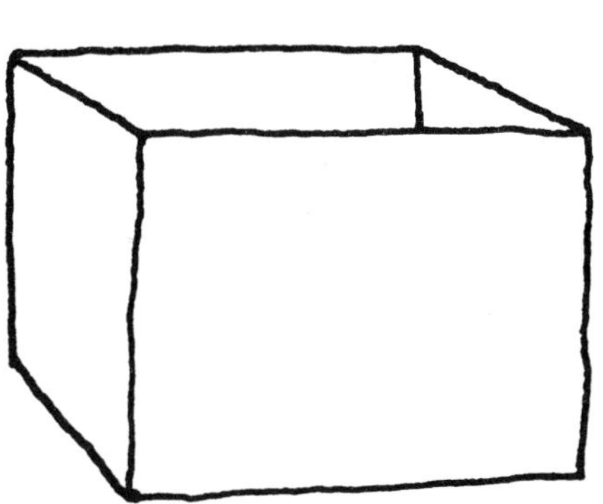
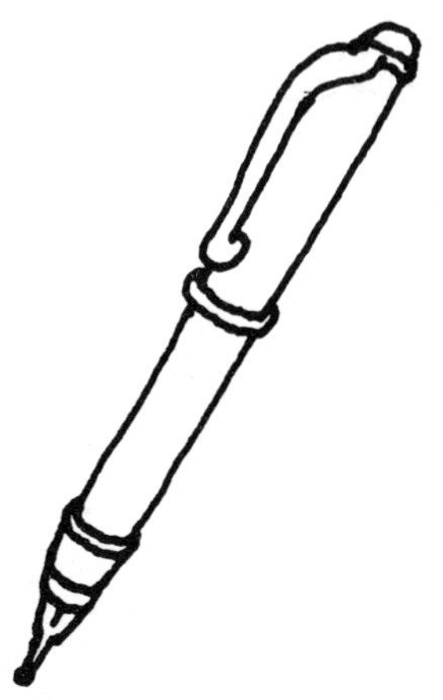
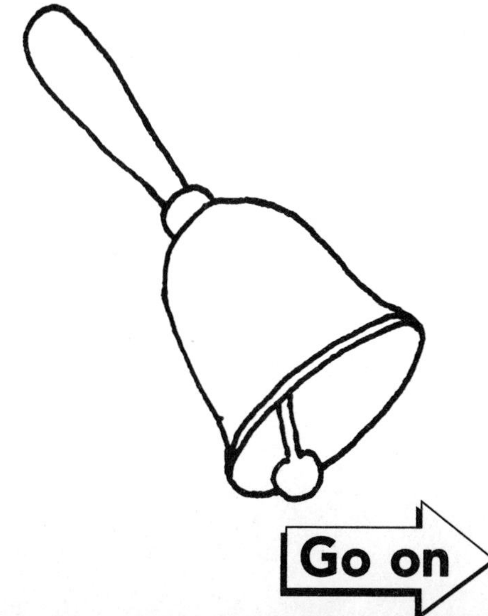

Go on

4.

5.

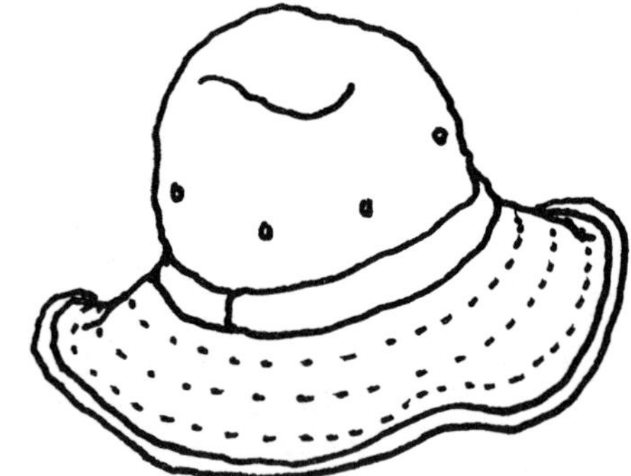

STOP

Part A Blending Phonemes ________

Name________________________________

Text Organization and Summarizing

1.

2.

3.

Part B Text Organization and Summarizing ________

Name________________________________

Cause and Effect

1.

2.

3.

Part C Cause and Effect ________

Name ______________________________

Initial Consonants: *h, v, c;* Blending Short *a* Words

1.

h

2.

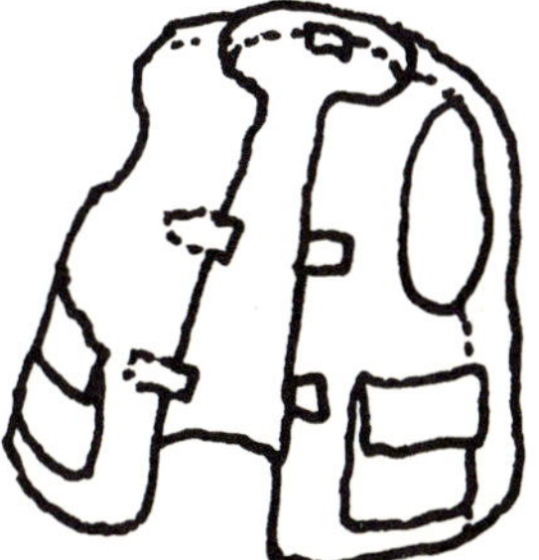

3.

c

STOP

Part D Initial Consonants: *h*, *v*, *c* ________

4. See my hat!

5. I see a cat.

Part D Blending Short *a* Words ________

Name ____________________

High-Frequency Words

1.

a

to

my

2.

to

like

a

3.

to

a

I

Part E High-Frequency Words: *a*, *to* ________

Let's Count!
Level K, Theme 5
Theme Skills Test Record

Student ______________________________ Date ________________

Test Record Form

PART	SCORE	LEVEL OF RESPONSE	RESULT S, D, E, or NE	COMMENTS
A Blending Phonemes (Maximum Score = 5)		4–5 = Strong 2–3 = Developing 1 = Emerging 0 = Not Evident		
B Categorize and Classify (Maximum Score = 3)		3 = Strong 2 = Developing 1 = Emerging 0 = Not Evident		
C Story Structure: Beginning, Middle, End (Maximum Score = 3)		3 = Strong 2 = Developing 1 = Emerging 0 = Not Evident		
D Initial Consonants: *p*, *g*, *f*; Blending Short *a* Words (Maximum Score = 5)		4–5 = Strong 2–3 = Developing 1 = Emerging 0 = Not Evident		
E High-Frequency Words: *and*, *go* (Maximum Score = 3)		3 = Strong 2 = Developing 1 = Emerging 0 = Not Evident		

Name____

Blending Phonemes

Practice

1.

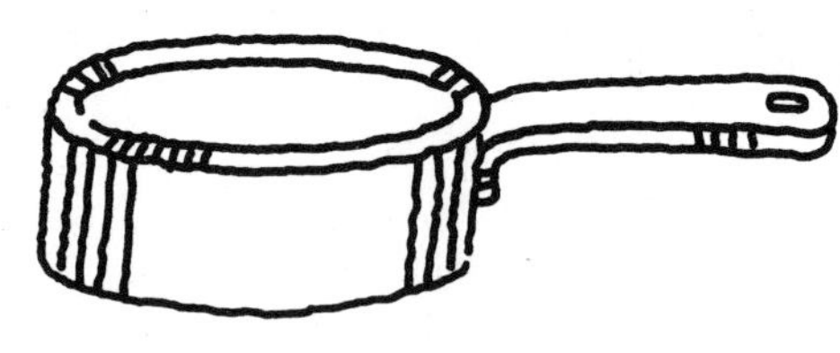

2.

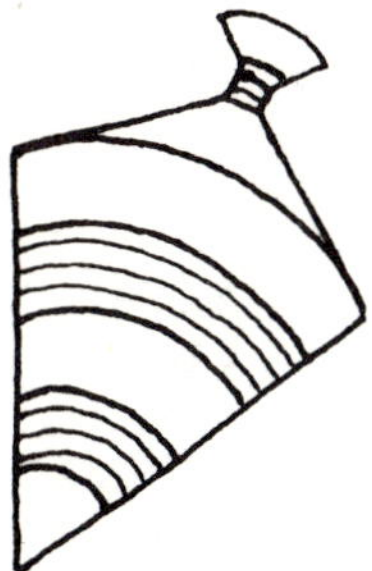

3.

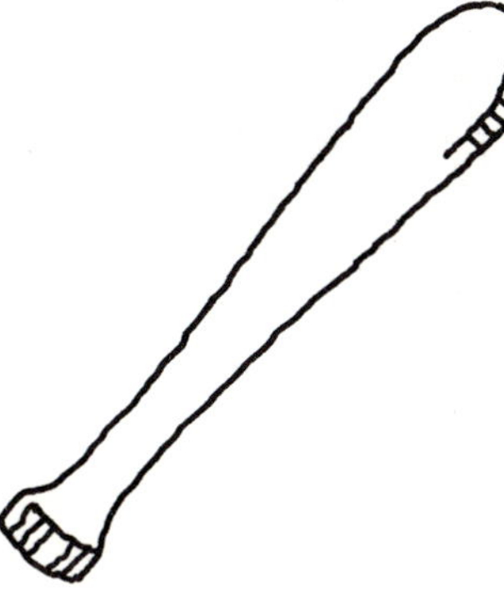

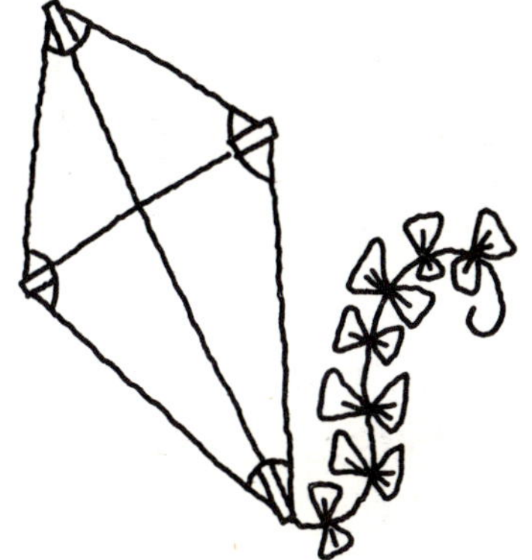

4.

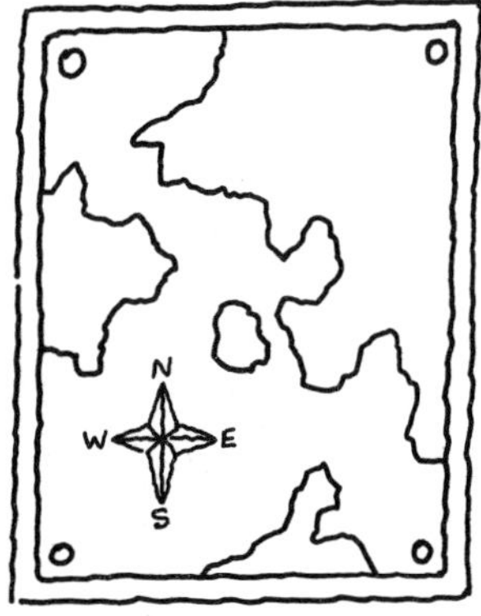

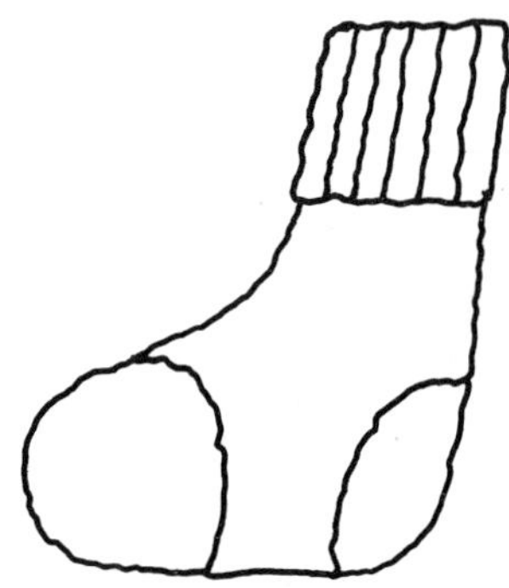

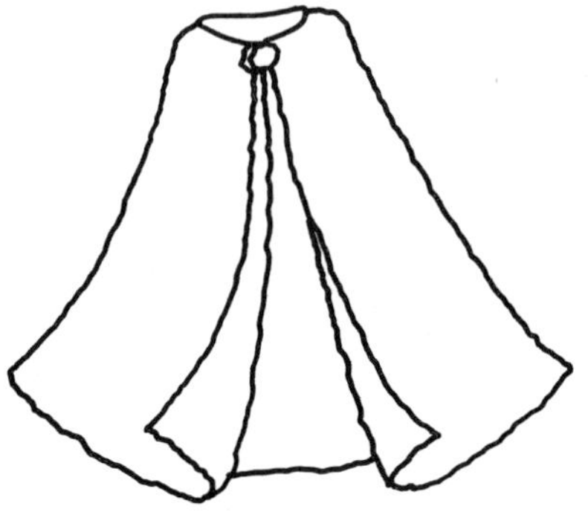

5.

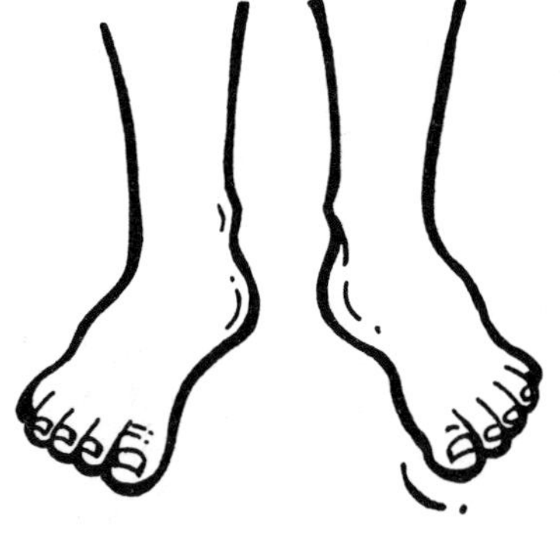

STOP

Part A Blending Phonemes ________

Name ____________________

Categorize and Classify

1.

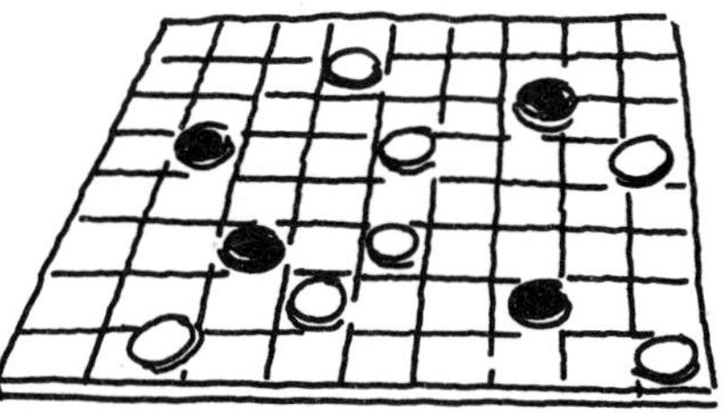

2.

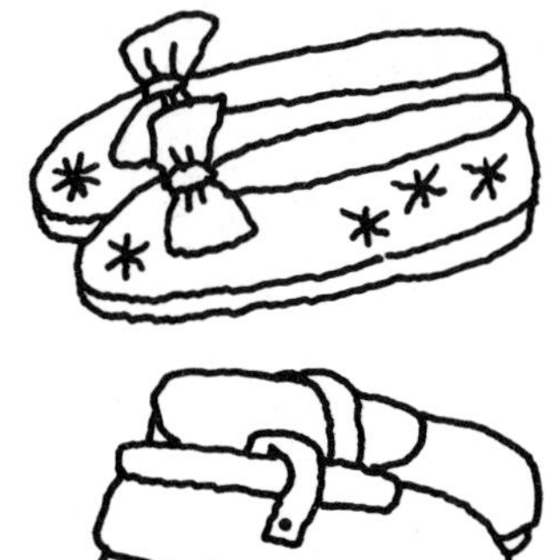

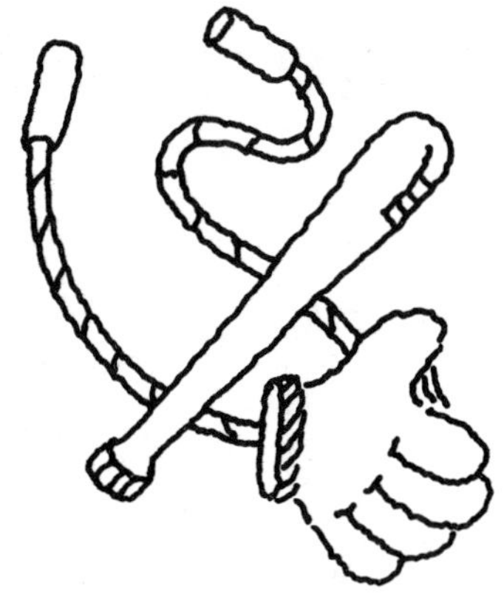

3.

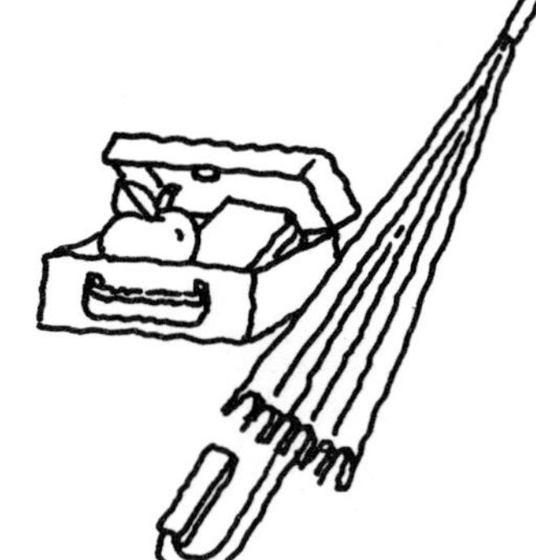

STOP

Part B Categorize and Classify ________

C

Name ______________________________

Story Structure: Beginning, Middle, End

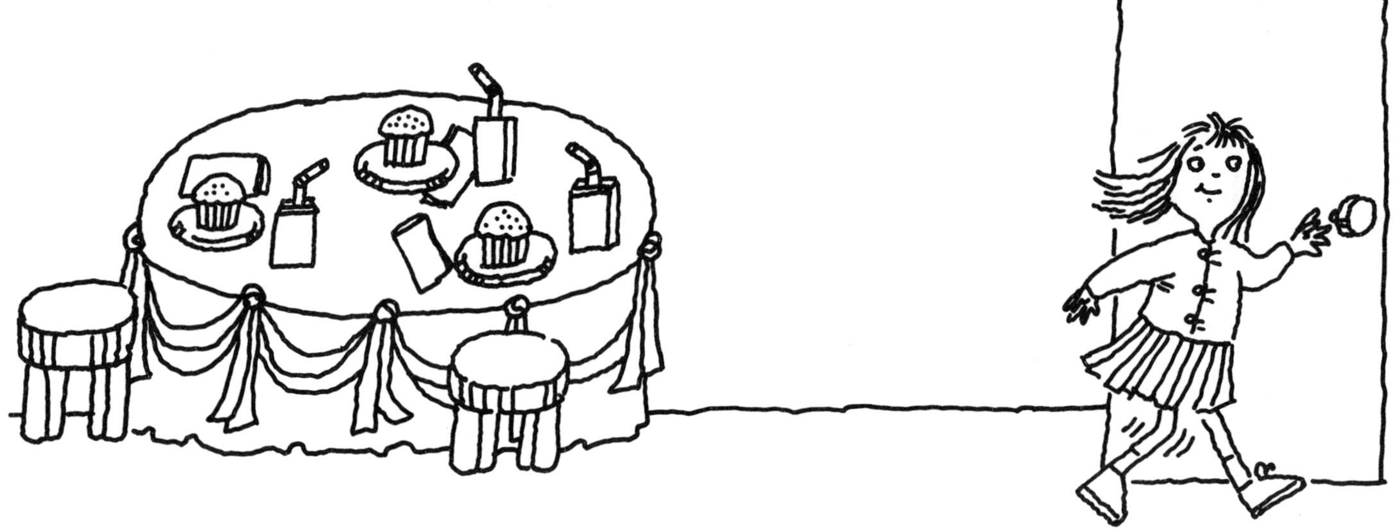

1.

2.

3.

STOP

Part C Story Structure: Beginning, Middle, End ________

Name ___________________________________

Initial Consonants: *p, g, f;* Blending Short *a* Words

1.

g

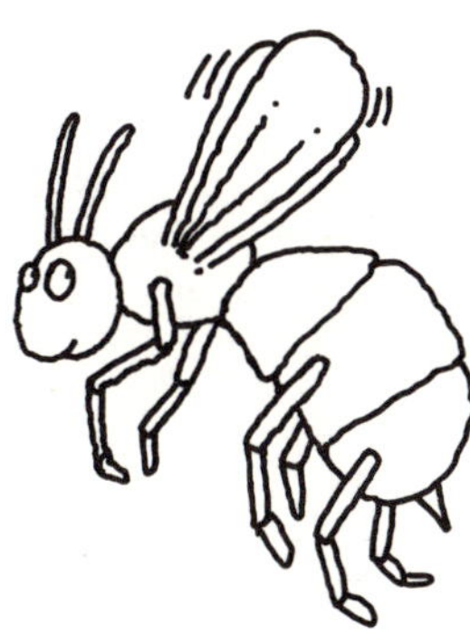

2.

p

3.

f

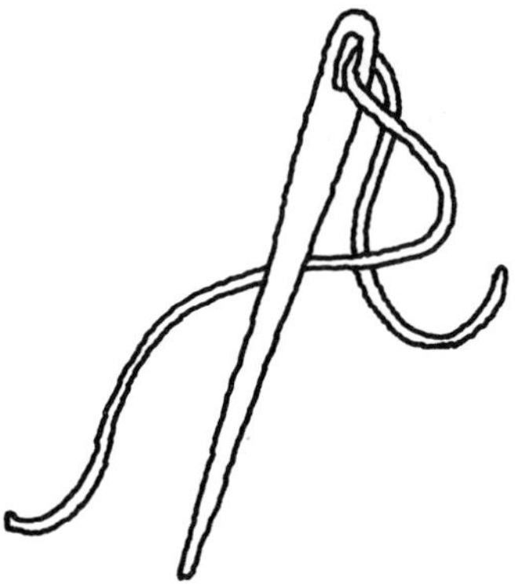

STOP

Part D Initial Consonants: *p*, *g*, *f* ________

4. Nat ran.

5. Nan and I see a man.

Part D Blending Short *a* Words ________

Name________________________________

High-Frequency Words

1.

go

like

and

2.

and

my

go

3.

and

go

a

Part E High-Frequency Words: *and*, *go* ________

Sunshine and Raindrops

Level K, Theme 6

Theme Skills Test Record

Student ______________________ Date ______________

Test Record Form

PART	SCORE	LEVEL OF RESPONSE	RESULT S, D, E, or NE	COMMENTS
A Blending Phonemes Segmenting Phonemes (Maximum Score = 5)		4–5 = Strong 2–3 = Developing 1 = Emerging 0 = Not Evident		
B Fantasy/Realism (Maximum Score = 3)		3 = Strong 2 = Developing 1 = Emerging 0 = Not Evident		
C Story Structure: Plot (Maximum Score = 3)		3 = Strong 2 = Developing 1 = Emerging 0 = Not Evident		
D Initial Consonants: *l, k, q;* Blending Short *i* Words (Maximum Score = 5)		4–5 = Strong 2–3 = Developing 1 = Emerging 0 = Not Evident		
E High-Frequency Words: *is, here* (Maximum Score = 3)		3 = Strong 2 = Developing 1 = Emerging 0 = Not Evident		

Name ____

Blending Phonemes

1.

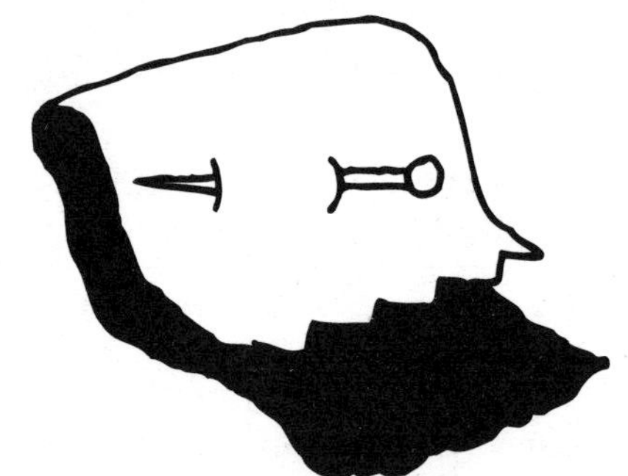

2.

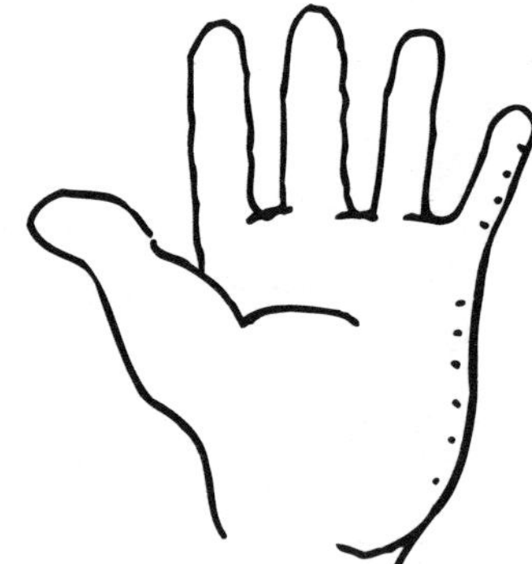

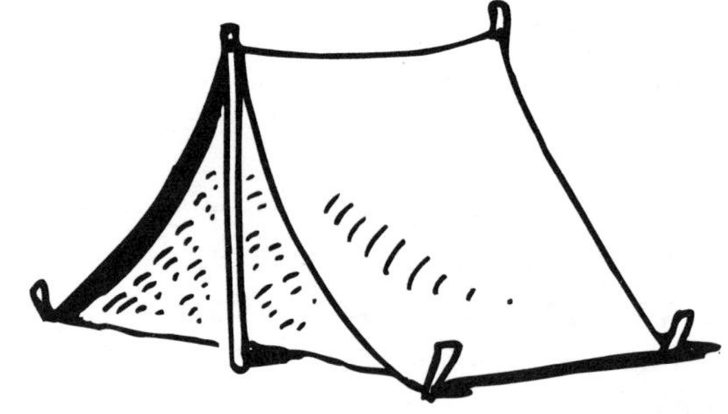

STOP

Part A Blending Phonemes ________

Segmenting Phonemes

Practice

3.

4.

5.

Part A Segmenting Phonemes ________

B Name ____________________

Fantasy/Realism

1.

Go on

2.

3.

Part B Fantasy/Realism ________

C

Name____

Story Structure: Plot

1.

2.

3.

STOP

Part C Story Structure: Plot ________

Name ______________________________

Initial Consonants: *l, k, q;* Blending Short *i* Words

1.

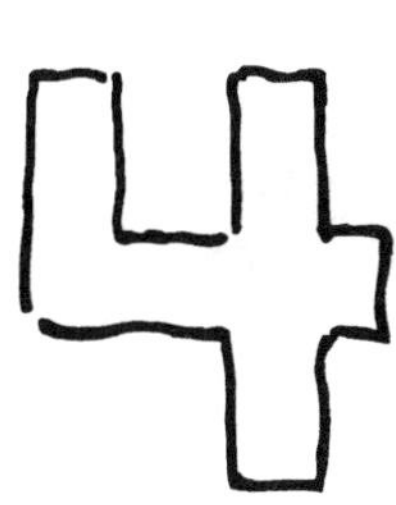

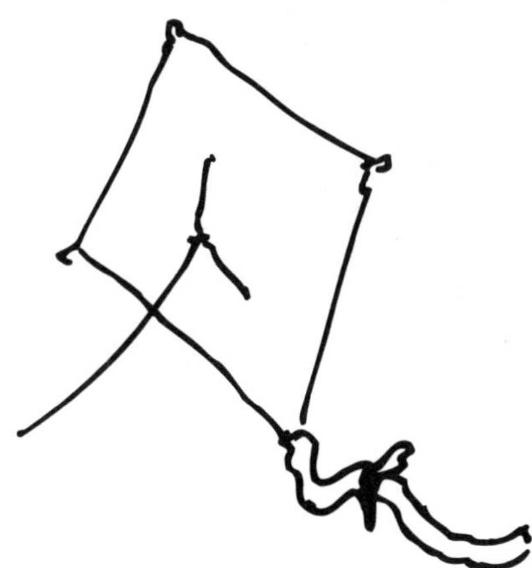

2.

3.

qu

STOP

Part D Initial Consonants: *l*, *k*, *qu* ________

4. Nan can sit here.

---

5. I like to hit it.

STOP

Part D Blending Short *i* Words ________

Name ______________________________

High-Frequency Words

1.

go

is

here

2.

is

my

here

3.

is

see

here

Part E High-Frequency Words: *is*, *here* ________

Wheels Go Around

Level K, Theme 7
Theme Skills Test Record

Student ______________________ Date ______________

Test Record Form

PART	SCORE	LEVEL OF RESPONSE	RESULT S, D, E, or NE	COMMENTS
A Blending and Segmenting Phonemes (Maximum Score = 5)		4–5 = Strong 2–3 = Developing 1 = Emerging 0 = Not Evident		
B Text Organization and Summarizing (Maximum Score = 3)		3 = Strong 2 = Developing 1 = Emerging 0 = Not Evident		
C Cause and Effect (Maximum Score = 3)		3 = Strong 2 = Developing 1 = Emerging 0 = Not Evident		
D Making Predictions (Maximum Score = 3)				
E Initial Consonants: *d*, *z*; Blending Short *i* Words (Maximum Score = 5)		4–5 = Strong 2–3 = Developing 1 = Emerging 0 = Not Evident		
F High-Frequency Words: *for*, *have* (Maximum Score = 3)		3 = Strong 2 = Developing 1 = Emerging 0 = Not Evident		

A Name______________________________

Blending and Segmenting Phonemes

1.

2.

Go on

3.

4.

Go on

5.  

Part A Blending and Segmenting Phonemes ________

B

Name ______________________________

Text Organization and Summarizing

1.

2.

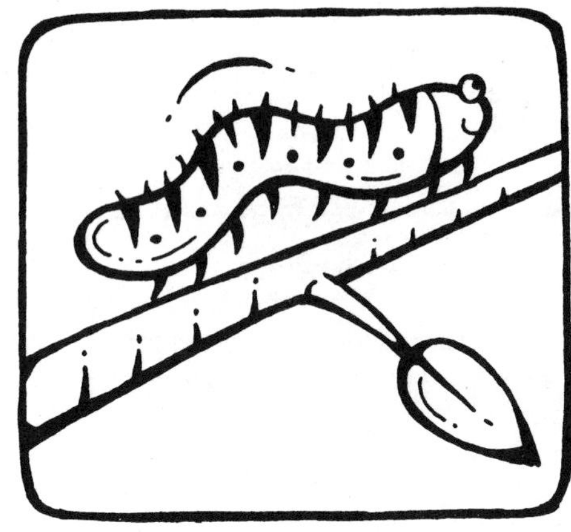

3.

Part B Text Organization and Summarizing ________

C

Name

Cause and Effect

1.

2.

3.

Part C Cause and Effect ________

Name ______________________________

Making Predictions

1.

2.

3.

STOP

Part D Making Predictions ________

Name________________________________

Initial Consonants: *d, z;* Blending Short *i* Words

1.

d

2.

z

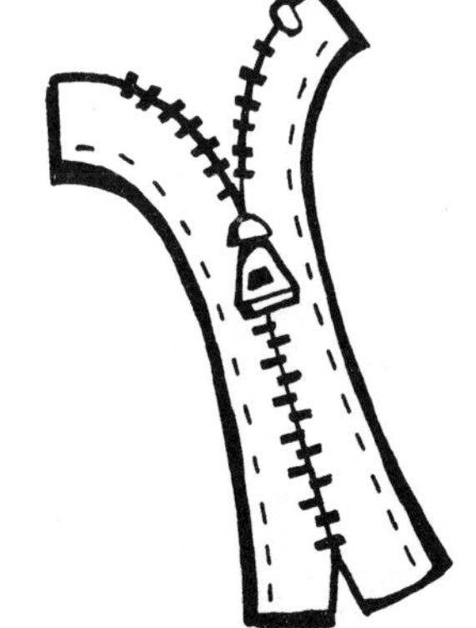

3.

d

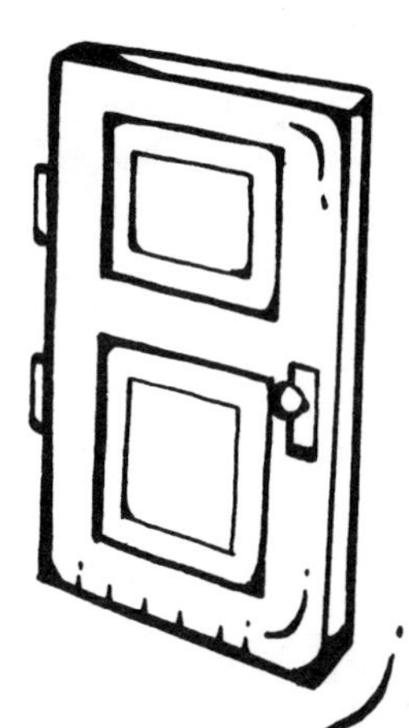

STOP

Part D Initial Consonants: *d*, *z* ________

4. Here is a big pig!

5. I see Nat dig.

Part E Blending Short *i* Words ________

Name____

High-Frequency Words

1\.

for

here

have

2\.

like

have

for

3.

have

to

for

Part F High-Frequency Words: *for*, *have* ________

Down on the Farm

Level K, Theme 8
Theme Skills Test Record

Student ______________________ Date ______________

Test Record Form

PART	SCORE	LEVEL OF RESPONSE	RESULT S, D, E, or NE	COMMENTS
A Blending and Segmenting Phonemes (Maximum Score = 5)		4–5 = Strong 2–3 = Developing 1 = Emerging 0 = Not Evident		
B Fantasy/Realism (Maximum Score = 3)		3 = Strong 2 = Developing 1 = Emerging 0 = Not Evident		
C Noting Important Details (Maximum Score = 3)		3 = Strong 2 = Developing 1 = Emerging 0 = Not Evident		
D Drawing Conclusions (Maximum Score = 3)				
E Final Consonant: *x*; Blending Short *o* Words (Maximum Score = 5)		4–5 = Strong 2–3 = Developing 1 = Emerging 0 = Not Evident		
F High-Frequency Words: *said*, *the* (Maximum Score =3)		3 = Strong 2 = Developing 1 = Emerging 0 = Not Evident		

Name

Blending and Segmenting Phonemes

1.

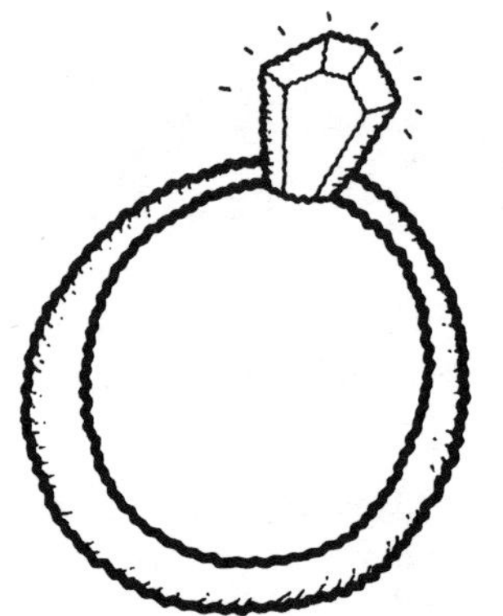

2.

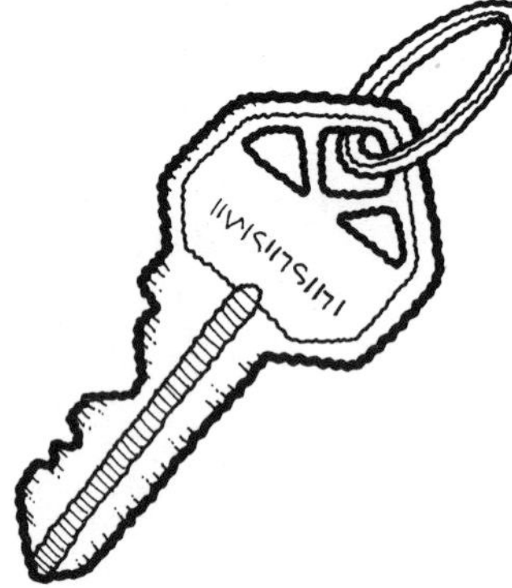

3.

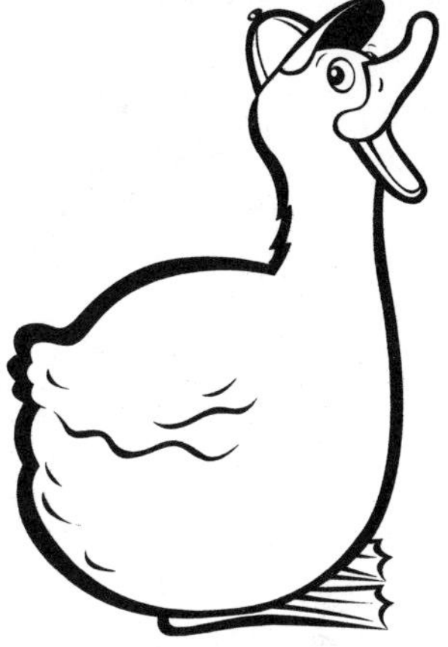

4.

5.

STOP

Part A Blending and Segmenting Phonemes ________

Name___________________________

Fantasy/Realism

1.

2.

3.

Part B Fantasy/Realism ________

C

Name________________________________

Noting Important Details

1.

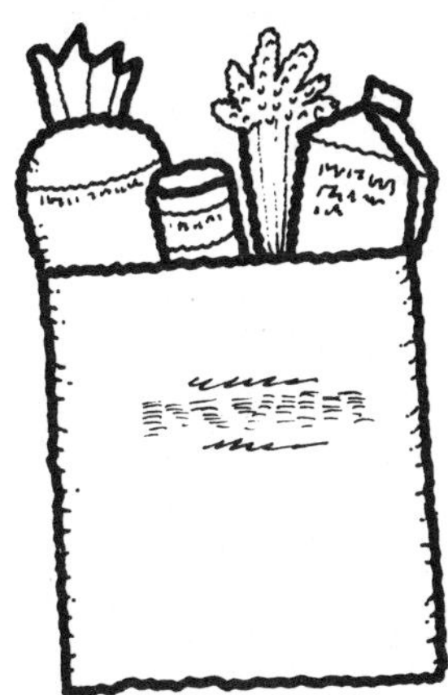

2.

3.

STOP

Part C Noting Important Details ________

Name____

Drawing Conclusions

1.

2.

3.

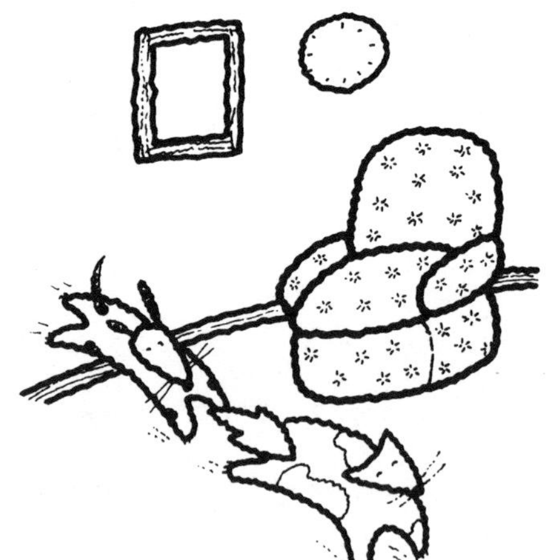

STOP

Part D Drawing Conclusions ________

Name_______________

Final Consonant: *x;* Blending Short *o* Words

1.

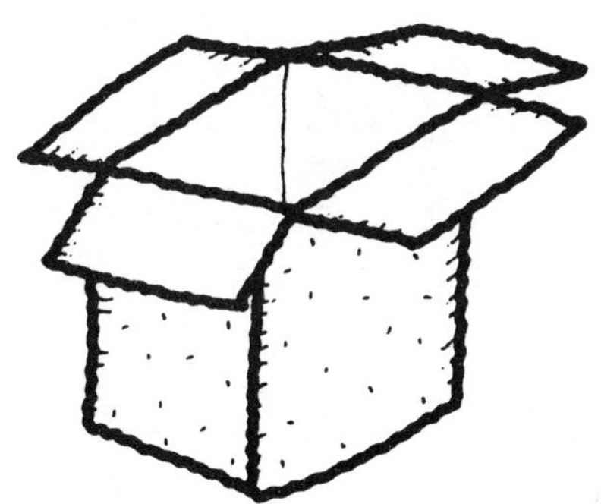

2.

STOP

Part E Final Consonant: *x* ________

3. Pat said, "It is hot here."

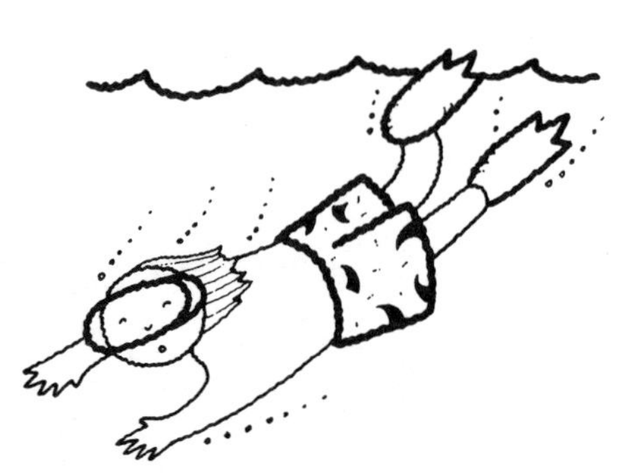

4. I like to see a big fox.

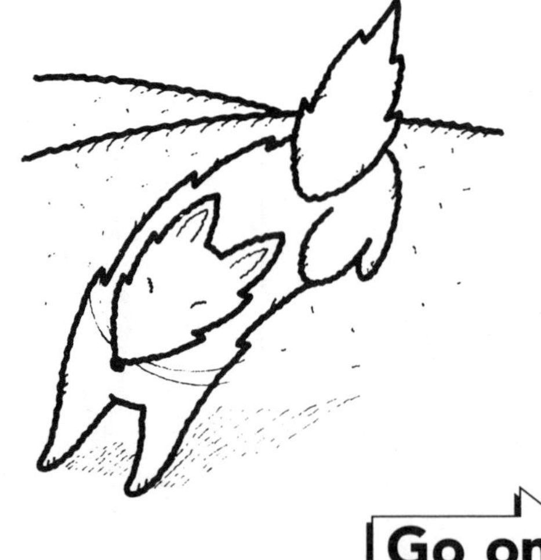

Go on

5. But the fox is <u>not</u> here.

Part E Blending Short *o* Words ________

F

Name ____________________

High-Frequency Words

1.

said

is

the

2.

the

said

and

3.

have

said

the

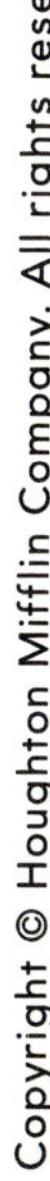

Part F High-Frequency Words: *said*, *the* ________

Spring Is Here

Level K, Theme 9

Theme Skills Test Record

Student ______________________ Date ______________

Test Record Form

PART	SCORE	LEVEL OF RESPONSE	RESULT S, D, E, or NE	COMMENTS
A Sequence of Events (Maximum Score = 3)		3 = Strong 2 = Developing 1 = Emerging 0 = Not Evident		
B Story Structure: Characters/Setting (Maximum Score = 3)		3 = Strong 2 = Developing 1 = Emerging 0 = Not Evident		
C Categorize and Classify (Maximum Score = 3)		3 = Strong 2 = Developing 1 = Emerging 0 = Not Evident		
D Initial Consonants: *w, y;* Blending Short *e* Words (Maximum Score = 5)		4–5 = Strong 2–3 = Developing 1 = Emerging 0 = Not Evident		
E High-Frequency Words: *play, she* (Maximum Score = 3)		3 = Strong 2 = Developing 1 = Emerging 0 = Not Evident		

A

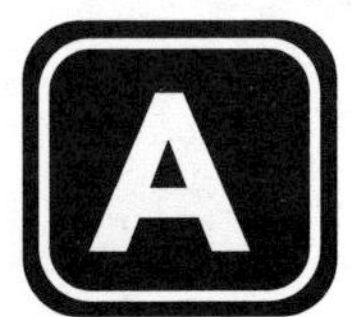

Name ____________________

Sequence of Events

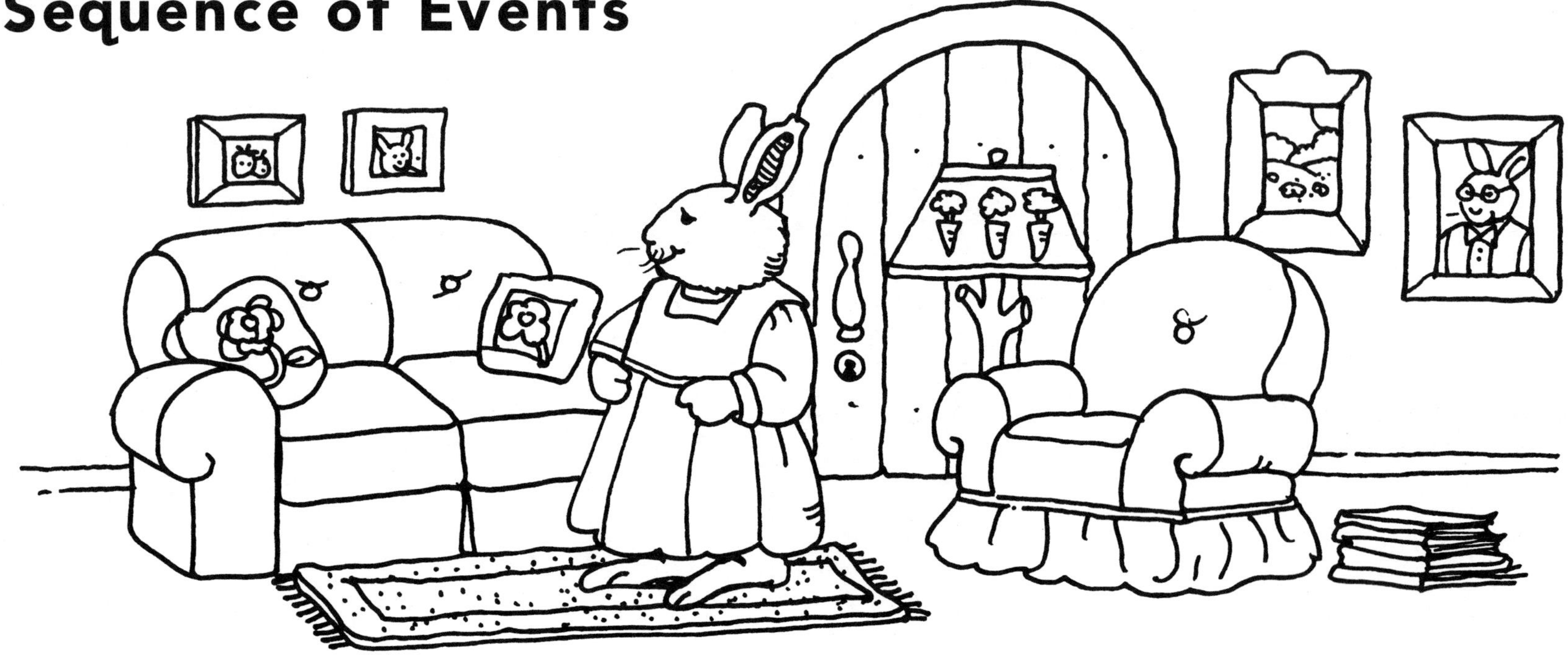

1.

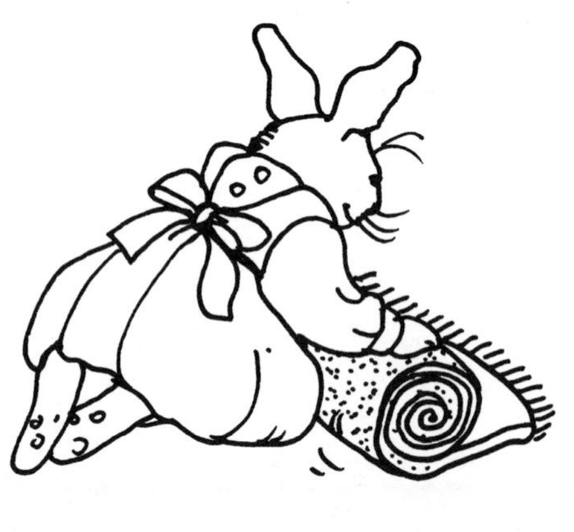

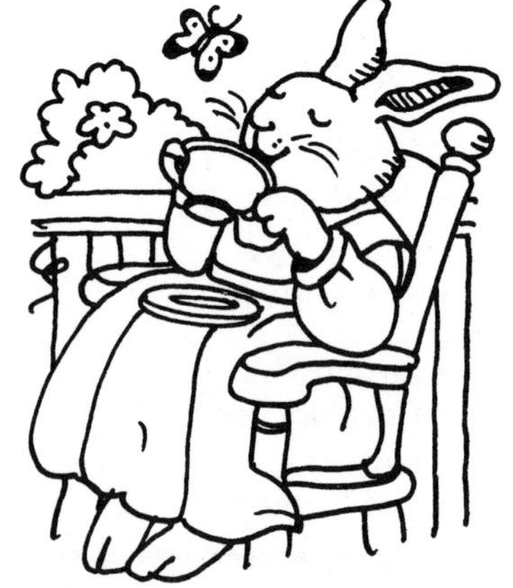

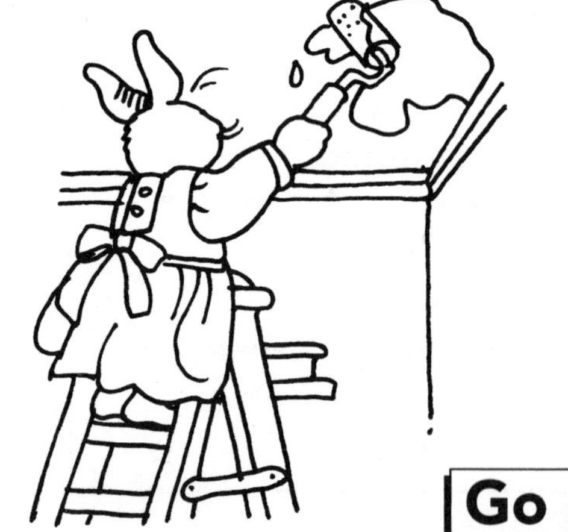

Go on

2.

3.

STOP

Part A Sequence of Events ________

Name____

Story Structure: Characters/Setting

1.

2.

3.

STOP

Part B Story Structure: Characters/Setting ________

Name______________________________

Categorize and Classify

1.

Go on

2.

3.

Part C Categorize and Classify ________

D Name

Initial Consonants: *w, y;* Blending Short *e* Words

1.

w

2.

y

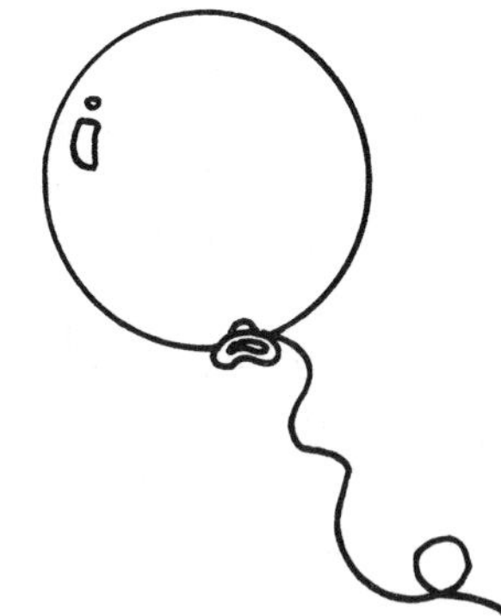

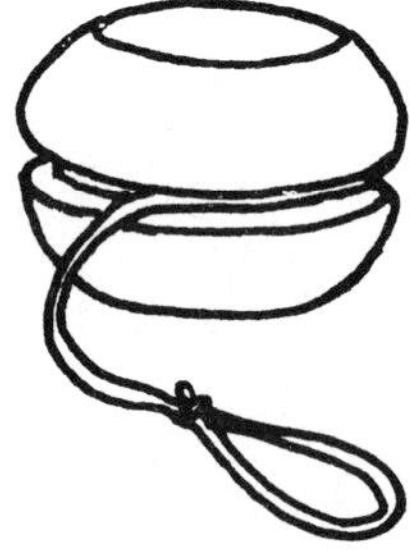

3.

w

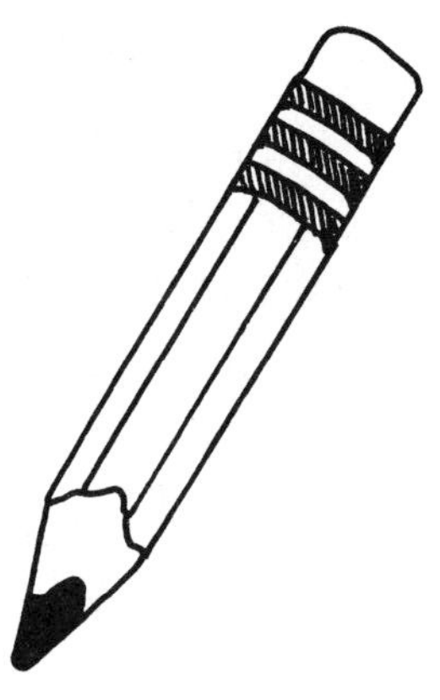

Part D Initial Consonants: *w*, *y* ________

4. I have a big pet <u>hen</u>.

5. It is hot. Nan and I get <u>wet</u>.

STOP

Part D Blending Short *e* Words ________

Name ____________________________________

High-Frequency Words

1.

play

go

she

2.

said

play

she

3.

she

and

play

STOP

Part E High-Frequency Words: *play, she* ________

A World of Animals
Level K, Theme 10
Theme Skills Test Record

Student ______________________________ Date ________________

Test Record Form

PART	SCORE	LEVEL OF RESPONSE	RESULT S, D, E, or NE	COMMENTS
A Story Structure: Beginning, Middle, End (Maximum Score = 3)		3 = Strong 2 = Developing 1 = Emerging 0 = Not Evident		
B Compare and Contrast (Maximum Score = 3)		3 = Strong 2 = Developing 1 = Emerging 0 = Not Evident		
C Story Structure: Plot (Maximum Score = 3)		3 = Strong 2 = Developing 1 = Emerging 0 = Not Evident		
D Initial Consonant: *j*; Blending Short *u* Words (Maximum Score = 5)		4–5 = Strong 2–3 = Developing 1 = Emerging 0 = Not Evident		
E High-Frequency Words: *are*, *he* (Maximum Score = 3)		3 = Strong 2 = Developing 1 = Emerging 0 = Not Evident		

Name ____________________

Story Structure: Beginning, Middle, End

1.

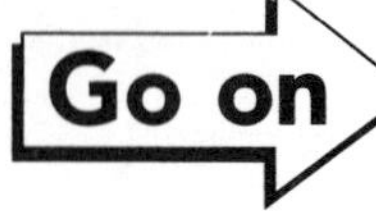

2.

3.

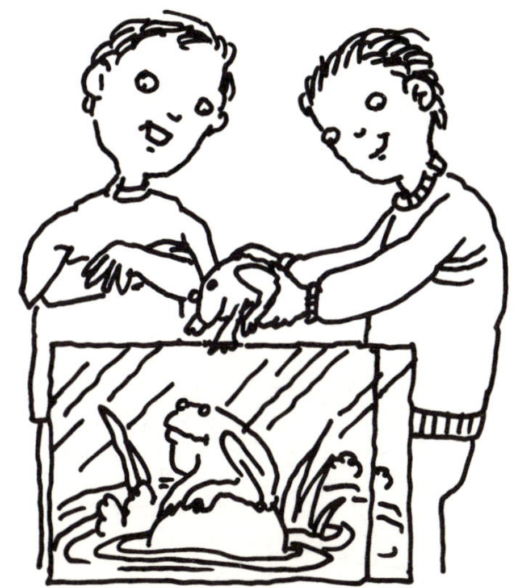

STOP

Part A Story Structure: Beginning, Middle, End ________

Name____

Compare and Contrast

1.

Go on

2.

3.

Part B Compare and Contrast ________

Name ____________________

Story Structure: Plot

1.

Go on

2.

3.

STOP

Part C Story Structure: Plot ________

D Name ____________________

Initial Consonant: *j*; Blending Short *u* Words

1.

2.

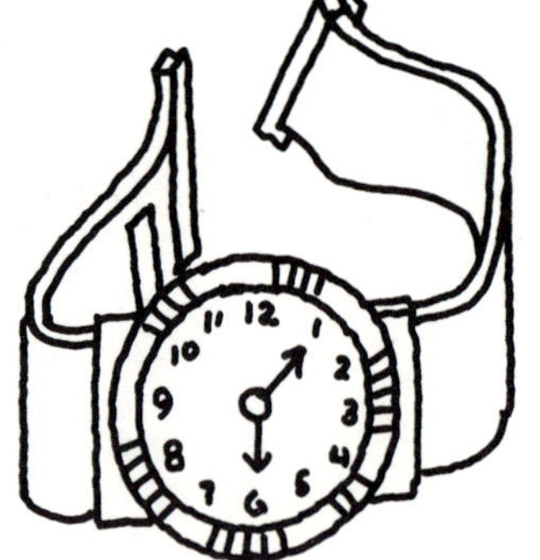

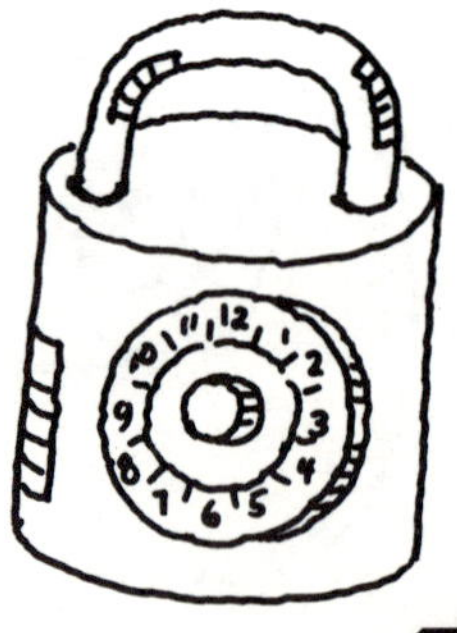

STOP

Part D Initial Consonant: *j* ________

3. See the <u>bug</u> go.

4. She can <u>cut</u> it.

Go on

5. I like to get a hug.

STOP

Part D Blending Short *u* Words ________

Name ______________________________

High-Frequency Words

1.

she

are

he

2.

he

go

are

Go on

3.

me

he

are

Part E High-Frequency Words: *are*, *he* ________